THE SUPER SHOPPER

# GETTING ORGANIZED

By Robyn Freedman Spizman
*Published by Ivy Books:*

GETTING ORGANIZED
KITCHEN 101
FREE AND FABULOUS*
SUPERMARKET SECRETS*
MEALS IN MINUTES*
QUICK TIPS FOR BUSY PEOPLE*

*\*Forthcoming*

Books published by The Ballantine Publishing Group are available at quantity discounts on bulk purchases for premium, educational, fund-raising, and special sales use. For details, please call 1-800-733-3000.

THE SUPER SHOPPER

# GETTING ORGANIZED

## Robyn Freedman Spizman

IVY BOOKS • NEW YORK

Sale of this book without a front cover may be unauthorized. If this book is coverless, it may have been reported to the publisher as "unsold or destroyed" and neither the author nor the publisher may have received payment for it.

An Ivy Book
Published by The Ballantine Publishing Group
Copyright © 1998 by Robyn Freedman Spizman

All rights reserved under International and Pan-American Copyright Conventions. Published in the United States by The Ballantine Publishing Group, a division of Random House, Inc., New York, and simultaneously in Canada by Random House of Canada Limited, Toronto.

Cover photo © Philip Shone Photography

http://www.randomhouse.com

Library of Congress Catalog Card Number: 97-94252

ISBN 0-8041-1682-2

Manufactured in the United States of America

First Edition: April 1998

10  9  8  7  6  5  4  3  2  1

This book is dedicated to you, the reader, for taking the plunge and getting organized. While it takes time and effort, the benefits are endless! To my brother Doug, who was born organized; to my sister-in-law Genie, who makes every wish come true; to my wonderful parents, Phyllis and Jack Freedman; my husband, Willy; and our children, Justin and Ali, for their unending love, support, and allowing me the time to organize my thoughts and ideas in order to write this book.

# Contents

| | |
|---|---|
| Acknowledgments | ix |
| Introduction: Getting Organized | 1 |
| 1. The Benefits of Getting Organized | 3 |
| 2. Organize Your Time First | 9 |
| 3. Unclutter Your Life | 17 |
| 4. Use Space-Saving Devices | 23 |
| 5. Get Organized by Themes | 29 |
| 6. Control the Paper | 33 |
| 7. Special Sections That Need Extra-Special Help! | 43 |
| 8. The Kitchen | 57 |
| 9. Other Areas Around the House | 65 |
| 10. Getting Your Family Organized | 71 |
| 11. Garage Sales | 75 |
| Epilogue: All's Well That's Organized Well | 79 |
| Index | 81 |

# Acknowledgments

Organizing a book is quite a large undertaking, and it couldn't have been done without the assistance of my organized editor, Elisa Wares, Laura Paczosa, and all the talented individuals at The Ballantine Publishing Group. A special thank-you also goes to my dedicated literary agent, Meredith Bernstein, to Bettye Storne for her valuable help in staying organized, and to Eileen Tropauer for her words of wisdom.

THE SUPER SHOPPER

# GETTING ORGANIZED

# Introduction: Getting Organized

Congratulations! You have just taken an important step toward getting organized by picking up this book. Whether you are chronically disorganized or an organizational whiz, *Getting Organized* will help put you or keep you right on track. Becoming organized is important, but staying organized is vital. The maintenance required is just minutes a day, but the payoff is huge! So even if you lack time or motivation, stick with me and I'll help you through those piles of papers and those cluttered drawers.

As a consumer expert, I have spent more than fifteen years reporting on how to get organized. It doesn't surprise me that this information is never outdated. Organization is a monumental job for most of us, but if you use my systematic approach, you'll divide and conquer your surroundings on your way to a less chaotic life. While the art of organization is a lifelong skill, my best advice is to take life one day at a time. Little things end up overwhelming us; misplacing one item or searching for a pen can drive us crazy. Chronic disorganization is stressful. Creating a manageable environment helps us save time, money, and sanity too!

As you read this book, stop and try the ideas in each chapter one at a time. Achieving an organized life can be fun and incredibly rewarding. You can turn an SOS into a Super Organized Space! When you free yourself of clutter, you also clear your mind and make more time for yourself as well as for others. Arm yourself with patience and set aside some time, because look out, clutter, here we come!

# 1

# The Benefits of Getting Organized

People are always asking me how I get so much done. As a busy mom and a professional working on numerous projects all the time, I have to be organized. I have set up simple systems for everything from clearing my desk to filing papers. I know just where to look to find my car keys, my reading glasses, or the scissors and tape. One of the greatest by-products of being organized is productivity. I can attest to the fact that being organized saves me time and allows me to get more done every day!

Being organized certainly contributes to the quality of your life. If you spend a great deal of your time looking for things you have misplaced or trying to get a grip on your affairs because they are not in order, then you often feel stressed out and overwhelmed.

How will getting organized help you? Getting organized will:

- save you time
- reduce stress
- make you feel more in control

- enhance and increase your productivity
- help you be more efficient

## Five Simple Secrets to Getting Organized!

The following five secrets will help you on the road to an organized life. That's right! You can free yourself of countless objects, pieces of paper, and things you really don't need. These rules work if you apply them to your home or office.

1. *Put time on your side.* Buy a daily planner or schedule book with a variety of add-ons—a calendar, an address book, and a notepad—and record all of your scheduled activities, plans, and meetings. If you prefer to write things down on a pocket calendar, that's fine, but organizing your time is as important as organizing your space. Next, schedule in a time to get organized! For some people, an hour over the weekend works best. Others prefer spending a little time in the morning or at the end of the day. To really get organized, you have to make organization a priority. You might even need a whole morning or day to get started, so take it. Don't let another week go by without making time to clean up your act!

## Rule 1. The best way to save time is to spend it getting organized.

2. *Less is best.* Take it one day at a time, or spend a weekend and go for it, but it's best to begin getting orga-

nized with a clean slate. When cleaning out a drawer or a cabinet, you must start from scratch. This means dumping everything out of the drawer or cabinet and starting over. Even if you start small, *start*. It also means trying on everything—yes, everything!—in your closet. Take everything out of the area you are cleaning, and if you don't use it, throw it out, recycle it, donate it, but get *rid* of it. Then clean the area you are organizing with a vacuum or a slightly damp cloth so that it is clean and ready to be organized. If you don't have time for the entire closet, take one section at a time.

> **Rule 2. You must scale down the number of things you own and own only the things you really need.**

3. *Use space-saving devices.* Ask yourself "What do I have a lot of?" If your closets or drawers are popping at the seams, either you have too much stuff or too little space. Perhaps you even have both! If you are short on space, organizational devices that are available today make getting organized a breeze. Measure the area you are working on and check out all the possibilities for such devices from hanging shelves to special clothing hangers or storage devices. Investigate each area of your environment and figure out where you could use some help. Visit a store that specializes in space-saving products and get inspired. In many cases, space-saving devices provide the foundation for getting and staying organized.

## Rule 3. Create an organized space and a place for everything you own or use.

4. *Get organized by themes.* By giving each drawer or cabinet a theme, you make the job of getting organized easier. For example, most of us have one drawer for knives, forks, and spoons. In it you probably have a drawer organizer (cutlery tray) separating them. Use this example for each drawer in your home; give each drawer a theme. (This rule also works for cabinets or closets depending on your space). What makes these drawer themes work is that everything must be returned to its proper space! Here are some obvious themes that work well:

- Office/home supply drawer: pens, notepads, scissors, tape, stapler, paper clips
- Stationery drawer: cards, notes, stationery, stamps
- Art supply cabinet: crayons, markers, paper, glue, glue sticks
- Junk drawer: the drawer for things that you aren't sure where to put, but want to save
- Address drawer: telephone books, address books

## Rule 4. Organize each space and return everything to its designated place.

5. *Take control of paper!* Paper is one of the hardest items to organize. But there is good news! Most paper can be easily reduced by over 50 percent. You must have

a system in place that makes it easy to keep track of important papers. When handling paper, remember: File it, don't pile it! Everyone needs a filing system at home and a place to store that system. Whether you purchase a small filing cabinet that fits under a counter or a plastic crate to store files in, you will need some sort of filing system. Keep a large supply of manila file folders and a marking pen stored in the front of the cabinet. Plus keep in mind: You must alphabetize files for your filing system to work!

### *Rule 5. Get rid of unwanted paper and file the rest.*

Now, are you ready to get organized? Clutter busters, read on! Those piles of paper and messy closets won't have a chance!

# 2

# Organize Your Time First

For organization to work, you have to work it into your life in an organized fashion. Perhaps you're wondering when you will find the time to get organized. Once you get in the habit of trying a few time-savers a day, you'll see that grabbing hold of your time is the best approach.

To begin getting organized, you'll need a clock in every major area where you work or spend time. Get in the habit of glancing at the clock when you begin a task and checking it again when you finish. Sometimes getting organized feels like it takes forever, but often it really only takes minutes. And there's good news! Getting organized ultimately helps you save time later on.

Organizing your time does require a bag of tricks. Time-savers really do work, and if you use them often, you'll be reinforced time and time again! The key to getting organized is to plan ahead. Head off those evenings when there's nothing in the freezer or pantry for dinner, or plan what you're going to wear so you won't discover your favorite shirt is still at the dry cleaner. Take charge of your time, and you'll see how easy it is to get more things accomplished and end up with time on your side!

## Timesaving Tips for Using Time Wisely

- Purchase a daily planner or schedule book. I consider this item something I can't live without. I prefer a looseleaf style book that I can customize and add pages to. I purchased a leather schedule book and have used it for years. My book zips up and has a few pockets for holding pens and business cards. I update this book yearly and have used the same system for quite a while. I like to see the entire month at a glance, and as I agree to or schedule an appointment, I record it the moment I learn about it. I also bought an extra holder for an alphabetical telephone directory.
- Make rules for yourself and then abide by them. For example, I always put my keys, my daily planner, and my purse in the same place. As long as I stick to this rule, I am able to find these items instantly.
- Check your schedule daily. A daily planner doesn't work unless you check it daily. Every morning and sometimes in the evening I will glance at my book for tomorrow's activities or for what's happening this week. Two things are sure. If I don't check my book, I am bound to miss something. And if I don't write down a message, I probably will forget it.
- Make it a rule to write *everything* down, from meetings to dentist and doctor appointments. As soon as you agree to be somewhere or do something, record that commitment in your daily planner. If you want to remember it, write it down!
- Check it off. Some people like to cross off the day in their schedule book after everything has been done.

This action gives a sense of accomplishment and keeps you focused on what's happening next. It also reinforces a good day's work.

- Underschedule one day. I like to underschedule one day a week, which gives me extra downtime for accomplishing odds and ends. It also makes me feel less overwhelmed when the going gets tough. Choose a day each week and try to avoid scheduling anything on that day. This is also a great day to spend some time getting organized.
- Prioritize your time. Everything is not life and death, and certainly some things can wait while others can't! So before you wear yourself out or put things off, consider what's most important to your life at that very moment. Spending time with your children is more important than emptying that dishwasher.
- Involve everyone in using time effectively. The entire family can assist with household chores and can contribute to the family in productive ways. Little ones can help you sort laundry, while setting the table and taking out the trash can be rotated among family members. Everyone should get into the act. The good news? You will have more time together as a family.
- Don't procrastinate. You'll save a lot of time if you don't put things off until later. Even if you can't complete a task, start it. A little done is better than none. When you get a message, if possible, respond to it that day or within a twenty-four-hour period. If you have a task that really needs to be done, do it as soon as possible. Remember this: In the time you've spent thinking

about doing something, you could have probably already accomplished it.

- Shop by catalog or telephone. In many cases, you can order gifts and even groceries by telephone. You can even call and have your dry cleaning picked up and delivered. Check out the resources and see when it pays to stay home. Catalog shopping is a wonderful way to save time and money. Find a few favorite dependable catalog stores and shop for gifts ahead of time. If some gift isn't suitable, then you'll have plenty of time to send it back.

- Request appointments with doctors and dentists at times that minimize the wait. In some cases, especially with dentists, the first appointment is the best one. Other times, it's ideal to be the first patient after lunch. Ask the receptionist what's the best time to get an appointment with as little waiting as possible and give it a try. Your time is valuable.

- Tired of meetings that go on forever? When scheduling a meeting, tell everyone exactly when you will be starting and ending the meeting, and you'll find everyone will respect the limits. This way your meeting won't drag on forever, and everyone will get right to the point!

- Schedule a breakfast, luncheon, or dinner meeting on a busy day when you don't have time to eat. This way you'll be doing two things at once and saving time on one!

- If time doesn't allow you to get something done and you find yourself putting it off, write yourself a re-

## GETTING ORGANIZED 13

minder on a self-stick note and place it somewhere obvious. When you finish the task, you get to remove the note.
- Make a list. To save time, keep self-stick notes and a pen by every telephone in your home. Keep these notes standing by, ready and waiting.
- Reward yourself! If a particular task is stressful to you, take a break after doing it.
- Plan your errands. Group errands at sites near each other to save time. You'll also save gas and energy. Consider what errands you do weekly. Dry cleaning? Groceries? Choose one day a week to do those errands and group them together when possible.
- While waiting at the doctor's office or in the car-pool line, bring something else to do. For example, balance your checkbook or read the mail.
- Wake up early. Give yourself extra time each day by waking up fifteen minutes earlier than everyone else. Use that time to get dressed, to organize your day, or even to read the newspaper. However you use the time, jump-start your day by starting off organized!
- When possible, do two things at once. Whether you polish your nails while you are on the telephone or flip through a magazine during television commercials, consider how you can do two activities simultaneously. One job well done is best, but when you can combine tasks, it's a great way to save time.
- Wear a watch. If you don't know what time it is, how can you manage your time effectively?
- Plan meals ahead of time. Each week give some

thought to meal planning. Think of a few basic standbys and have the ingredients on hand. Don't forget freezer pleasers—dinners available on demand!

- When purchasing ingredients for a favorite recipe, stock up on the individual items in it. You're bound to buy them again and again, and you can save yourself some time by getting extras.
- Learn to say no. If you are feeling overwhelmed, limit your activities. This doesn't mean you have to say no to everything. Just prioritize and say yes only to things you feel you can accomplish without compromising yourself and the task. Sometimes it helps to limit your no to a specific period of time: "I'm not able to help out this month, but please feel free to involve me next month."
- Clean up as you prepare and serve a meal and you won't end up with a big job for dessert! If you wait until dinner is over to clean everything up, it takes more time and energy.
- Work smart! Before you do an errand or a chore, consider the best way to do it. Don't be impulsive; instead, think about how you are using your time.
- Shop during less busy times. Grocery shopping is best done early in the morning—let's say, 8:30 A.M.—you'll save time by not having to wait in lines. If stores are less crowded at opening or closing times, shop accordingly. Late afternoon and lunchtime are usually the busiest times for most stores, but each store is unique, so get to know the best time to shop!
- No time left for you? Perhaps you feel like you have time for everyone and everything else. Well, it's time

to take care of you. Everyone will be better off and so will you. Don't fail to exercise because there's no time; instead, consider fitting in fitness in small increments each day. Take a full-fledged lunch break every day; carry along a paperback or magazine for waiting times. You deserve it!

- Call first. Before you make an unnecessary trip, check to make sure someone's home, your item is in stock, or an office is open.
- Investigate the different telephone answering options you have. The telephone company offers many new timesaving options, from message retrieval when you aren't at home to gadgets that even let you know who's on the line. Decide what features will assist you and try them out.
- Adopt the rule today that *doing it yesterday is better*. Try and do as much as you can each day, and you'll find tomorrow easier. Ask yourself, "Can it wait?" and decide if there are any consequences for putting it off.
- For jobs that take longer, such as paying bills or going through mail you have ignored, choose a day when you have a block of time to get the job done. Get in the habit of finishing the job, or it will go on forever.
- When you are really busy and don't have any time, be honest with your friends and family. Share with them your time limitations and plan ahead. If you can't be interrupted or are bogged down with too much to do, let all of them know what to expect and how they might help you.
- Save time by creating a gift closet. Have a selection of gifts and items on hand. Stock up on a few greeting

cards as well, and you'll be ready when you need one quickly.
- Need a gift sent immediately? Check out the Yellow Pages and local resources and find companies that can rise to the occasion, no matter what it is! Options range from cakes to fruit baskets. This way you'll be ready for gifts you have to send in a flash!

Now that you have some extra time . . . spend it getting organized!

# 3

# Unclutter Your Life

Reducing the amount of clutter in your life is hard, but crucial. Face it, the more you have to organize, the more difficult your job will be. So call in the clutter patrol to forge ahead and face the masses of things we save to do on a rainy day. You'll be so glad you did! Often these things end up in the basement or stockpiled in a closet, but wherever they are, you must unclutter your life. This chapter will assist you in taking on this task one day, closet, or drawer at a time. Often people fail in getting organized because they can't reduce their clutter. Take it from me, you don't need it and less is best!

I've said this in the previous section, but the rules are worth repeating.

## The Basic Steps for Uncluttering Your Life

1. *Take it one day at a time.* Whether you choose a day a week for one month or an hour a day, you must make an agreement with yourself to start getting organized. Take one drawer, closet, or area of your house and empty it

out. That's right, dump that drawer, pull everything out of the closet, or take everything off the counter and out of the cabinet. Wipe out the area so that it's clean and dry and then decide what you really need to have in that drawer or closet. Read chapter 4 about space-saving devices and themes and apply my system to your life.

2. *Throw it out or give it away.* Ask yourself as you face all of your stuff: "Do I really need it, or does it just take up space? What am I saving it for? How long have I had it? When was the last time I used or wore it?" If you've had it a year and haven't used it in that time, then you probably don't need it or you will never use it. You *must* eliminate objects and reduce clutter in order to get organized.

3. *Practice using the circular file.* The circular file is the trash can, plain and simple. The wastebasket or recycling bin is the perfect solution to reducing clutter. The circular file is the perfect place for dried-up paints, papers you really don't need to save, or old correspondence that is no longer necessary. It's ready and waiting!

4. *Use the shopping-bag trick.* Hang a shopping bag on the back of the door to every closet in your home. Whenever you spot an item in the closet that you no longer need, put it into the bag. Some people like starting out this way, while others attack closets head-on. The shopping-bag trick works for long-term uncluttering and will help you reduce the number of things you own and don't really need.

## GETTING ORGANIZED

5. *Choose a worthwhile cause to donate these items to.* I donate items I no longer want to a good cause or someone who needs them. Look in your yellow pages under Social and Human Services or Charitable Organizations and you'll find quite a few that will pick up your nearly new and sometimes even very used belongings and household items.

6. *Know what you own and what you need.* Have you ever found yourself purchasing something you already own? Or perhaps you end up with too much of everything because you always think you have run out? Survey your closets, drawers, and cabinets and do a reality check before you shop.

7. *Don't buy it unless you really need it and have a place to put it!* Next time you go to add something material to your life, ask yourself, "Do I really need this item?" Then ask yourself, "Where will I put it?" Ask if the item you are buying is returnable and save your receipt. Sometimes we buy something for the pure thrill of purchasing it or because it was a bargain. All that does is build up the clutter and waste money. Resist the urge.

### Tips for Uncluttering Your Life

- You need to cut down on the amount of clutter in your world. Consider what you deal with daily. Too much stuff? Tons of junk mail? Too many credit cards? Papers galore? Explore ways to reduce the number of things you own. Be a clutter buster.

- Have a place and a space for everything. If you keep items that you use regularly in the same place, they are less likely to get lost. This also helps you see what you own.
- Clean things up regularly. Go through your in- or out-box daily. Don't let things pile up. Whether it's a magazine or a piece of mail, make sure you put it where it belongs. Refer to chapter 6 on getting control of the paper in your life.
- If you haven't used it in the past year, give it away or throw it out! Don't keep things for a rainy day. I promise you, the rain won't come! If you absolutely can't part with something for sentimental reasons, put it in a plastic airtight storage box under your bed. In the years to come, you'll either be thrilled you saved it or wonder whatever possessed you!
- Too many books? Donate them to a library, a home for the aged, a nonprofit book sale, or a local shelter. Too many toys? Find a homeless shelter or a child-care center that will appreciate them. Too many clothes? Two options are clothing resale stores and thrift shops for good causes. Decide if you want a tax write-off or the opportunity to make money off your used clothing. Check out the options in your community.
- Reduce junk mail by requesting the removal of your name from junk-mail lists. Write a letter requesting this to the Direct Marketing Association. Include a self-addressed, stamped envelope and request the appropriate form. Its address is:

Mail Preference Service
Direct Marketing Association
P.O. Box 9008
Farmingdale, NY 11735-9008

- If you're a pack rat, group like things together. If you save journals or papers, buy something that will keep the items together. I have found that loose-leaf notebooks and a hole puncher come in handy when saving materials that are alike. Simplify your life by putting related items together.
- Store items you handle often in clear folders. Purchase six clear-plastic envelopes, decide what will go in each, and label each with a permanent marking pen. For example, one envelope can be for coupons, another for address books, etc. My theory is, if you can see what you have, you'll know where to find it. Clean out the envelopes on a regular basis.
- Create clutter catchers. If you find you still have no place to put things, put a few baskets around your home to act as clutter catchers. For example, add a magazine basket to the room you live in most. This can be a decorative touch if you keep it organized. Save the magazines you can't part with, and give away the rest.
- Make room for new items. Live by the rule that whenever you buy something or receive something new, you must get rid of something else.
- Make space for holiday gifts by cleaning out your closets. Also consider cleaning out your closets four times a year. Follow the seasons—fall, winter, spring, and summer. This works especially well for a child—

before a birthday or special holiday when you know gifts are on their way.
- Clear off the counters. No matter how clean or messy your living spaces are, if the counters are cluttered, the room will look even more disorganized. So attack the counters first, clearing off the piles and relocating the items that have built up.

# 4

# Use Space-Saving Devices

One of my favorite ways to get organized is to use space-saving gadgets and systems. For some instant inspiration, visit a store in your area that specializes in space-saving items. These really work, and if you are dedicated to getting organized, plan on checking them out.

Here are some of my favorites:

- *Plastic-coated shelving.* This type of open shelving is covered in a white rubberized plastic and is easy to clean. While it comes in precut shelves scaled to fit a variety of objects including cleaning supplies and more, it is also sold by the yard so that it can be custom-fit to hold shoes, clothing, and other items. It is ideal for:

Interior sides of cabinets
Pantry and cabinet doors
Medicine cabinets
Under-the-sink cabinets
Shoe racks in closets

Closet shelves or racks
Shelving for garage tools

- *Cabinet-door paper towel holder.* Every home must have one in the kitchen! Don't leave the store without checking the length of the screws included in the package. If your cabinet door is thin, you'll need shorter screws to attach the holder.
- *Over-the-door hangers.* These are great for hanging clothes after they are ironed or for hanging up clothes you are going to wear the next day.
- *Double hangers.* Want to save some space? These hangers allow you to hang two items together in what would normally be the space of one. They're great for maximizing your space.
- *Under-the-bed storage boxes.* Out of sight, out of mind—this is the best way to store clothing or special items. Check every few months to make sure no moisture has gotten in your box, and store only clothing that is totally clean.
- *Bins and baskets.* These increase storage space, especially in closets and pantries. Bins and baskets offer you a functional way to store food, toys, and objects of all kinds. They are also great for recycling items, and many come with lids and in a variety of colors.
- *Lazy Susans.* A lazy Susan makes it easy to see just what's on the other side. This is a definite addition to any cabinet that needs to hold a lot of items such as spices, sugar, salt, or even medicine bottles.

- *Pull-out shelves.* Install these when you need to have full view of what's in the cabinet. Pull-out shelves make everything easier to reach and locate. A surefire hit for place mats, pots and pans, plastic containers, and so forth.
- *Grid system.* Store your favorite utensils, garden supplies, and tools on a grid system without cluttering a countertop. They are perfect for garages or anyplace you have lots of objects and extra wall space.
- *Clear storage containers.* Clear is best when it comes to storing multiples of items such as food, sewing materials, and so forth. See-through containers help you find it fast and are reusable over the years.
- *Colorful plastic holders.* Colorful plastic containers and holders serve as a handy way to store objects from magazines to toys and craft supplies. They can also add a bright touch to a playroom or closet that needs a little help.

## Using Space-Saving Organizers

- Get to know the products available. Visit a store and ask a salesperson for help. Discuss your specific problems and get the facts on what items are available to help you.
- Measure the areas you are organizing. Know how deep and wide your cabinets are and the exact dimensions of your drawers. You'll save time if you have the measurements with you when you shop.

- Think about what your biggest organizational problem is. Start there and take on only one area at a time.
- If your kitchen pantry is overflowing with canned goods, take everything out of the cabinet and see what you really don't use or need. Before purchasing extra can holders or more shelves, notice what you have the most of. Are you always stocking up on a particular item? Keep a shopping list to help cut down on buying for the sake of buying.
- Use storage devices properly. For example, assign specific spots in a can holder to specific types of canned goods. When there is an empty spot in the can holder, you'll know what you need to purchase. Remember, too much of a good thing is no longer good!
- Hire a professional. If you are overwhelmed and can't make your space work, consult with a company that specializes in closet and cabinet planning. Choose a reputable company with a successful track record and check out their work. Make sure they work from a plan and you know exactly what you are getting.
- It worked for me! Talk to your most organized friends and share ideas. Almost everyone has at least one great organizational tip. Ask your friends and family what theirs are, and which devices they have installed in their homes.
- Purchase furniture that's functional. Storage and shelving systems can be decorative in appearance and also of great help. For example, an armoire in our house holds a television set, extra clothing, videotapes, and even some of my favorite magazines. Consider decorating

with a purpose so your furniture contributes to your organizational needs.
- Purchase clear organizers, from canisters to envelopes. If you can see what's inside, organizing is simpler.

# 5

# Get Organized by Themes

A great technique for organizing is to arrange objects and clothing by themes, and sometimes by color. Themes are easily remembered and make organization easier. Thematic drawers should also be located where they are used most often, and items that are used together should be grouped together. Here are some useful themes for drawers, cabinets, or closets.

### In the Kitchen

- Office/home supply drawer (sometimes called a scissors drawer): pens, notepads, scissors, tape, stapler, paper clips
- Art cabinet, drawer, or closet: great for children's materials, including crayons, markers, paper, glue, glue sticks, odds and ends
- Address drawer: telephone books, address books, directories
- Silverware
- Kitchen utensils

- Pots and pans
- Cups
- Coffee mugs and teacups

## In the Bedroom

- Emergency drawer: nighttime necessities, flashlight, pen, notepad, emergency numbers
- Stationery drawer: notes, pen, notepad, special address book

## In the Bathroom

- Makeup drawer
- Hair dryer drawer
- Jewelry drawer
- Medicine cabinet
- Toilet paper cabinet

## Tips for Organizing by Themes

- Check out all the organizational devices that are designed for specific items. Organizers range from jewelry boxes to pencil and CD holders. They provide the structure and incentive to get organized.
- Make sure the devices work. To maximize your efficiency, check items from pens to staplers out often.

## GETTING ORGANIZED 31

Make sure objects are ready to be used and serve a purpose.
- Don't go back to your old habits. The second you start mixing themes and combining odds and ends, your drawers will become a lost cause.
- Enforce a put-it-back rule. Thematic storage spaces work only when you *put back* what you have taken from the drawer, closet, or cabinet. This rule must apply for the entire family! If you use it and lose it, what good is it? Make sure everyone knows the rules of the game.
- Use drawer dividers. Dividers help most drawers get and stay organized.

# Control the Paper

Paper is one of the biggest organizational challenges and must be dealt with head-on. To control the flow of paper in your house, you must create a system that deals with it strategically. The best way to handle paper is to get rid of as much of it as possible and to file those things that you absolutely must keep.

The following five types of paper require a plan for dealing with them. You must decide what you are going to do with each type and be aware of the different ways that paper must be organized.

| **Type of Paper** | **Where It Should Go** |
| --- | --- |
| Paper that must be read | Magazine basket, in and out wire or plastic tray on your desk, in a folder marked To Do. |
| Paper that must be filed | In file folders in a filing cabinet or plastic crate. |
| Paper that must be paid | In a file folder marked Pay or in a special basket on your desk. |

| | |
|---|---|
| Paper that must be saved | Each item saved must be put in a specific drawer, storage system, plastic container, folder, or other place. |
| Paper that must be discarded | Head directly into the wastebasket, do not pass Go! |

## Choose a Place to Handle Paper

Designate a workspace where you will handle paper. Some people actually divide this activity between the kitchen table and their desk at work or at home. Wherever you choose to deal with paper, create a space that has all the tools, files, and types of paper nearby. Some people store all of their files or paper in a particular closet and bring them out as necessary.

## Important Materials and Tools for Handling Paper

- In-box (for things that need to be dealt with)
- Out-box (for items or mail that must be paid, mailed, or given to someone)
- File cabinet or crate, one that works for your designated space
- File folders
- Business card organizer
- Calendars, one master and one personal that travels with you
- Stapler and staple remover
- Extra pens, pencils, and sharpener

- Stamps
- Correction fluid and correction tape
- Stationery supplies: postcards, note cards, return address labels
- Post-it notes (wonderful for quick notes)
- Rolodex system and lots of blank cards
- Tape
- Scissors
- Paper clips
- Rubber bands
- Wastebasket
- Recycling container

### Create a Filing System

Filing systems are one of the most efficient ways to take charge of paper. You need to create easy-to-remember names for the files so that you can locate them later. The name of a file should be a noun or proper noun.

**Easy-to-Remember File Names**
Bank account
Camp
Children (a file for each child by name)
Computer
Credit cards
Decorating
Donations
Entertainment

Health
Home improvement
Insurance
Legal documents
Letters
Medical
Property
Schools
Taxes
Travel
Valuables
Warranties

While there are many other headings that will apply to your life, the most important thing is to consider what papers you must save most often and then create specific files for them. I keep a box of manila file folders handy just in case I need a new file category. I prefer standard paper folders, and I buy them in bulk so as to have plenty on hand.

## How to Make Your Files Function

- File it, don't pile it! You must—I repeat, must—have a filing system for the important papers you save daily. Your filing system will not work unless you arrange it in alphabetical order.
- Make the filing tabs clear and easy to find. Use a black pen or permanent marker to write on the file names. Be sure to file things by a name you will remember. On the

first file folder, write down important file names that you might forget!
- Have a file for each family member, and keep important records (for example, birth certificates, passports, marriage license) in a safe or metal box for safe storage.
- Avoid miscellaneous files, which quickly become junk files holding things you never remember you have. If you can't classify the piece of paper, then forget about saving it!
- Keep a few of your most-often-used files either at the front of the filing system or in a basket on your desk. If you use them every day or two, this technique will save you time.
- File warranties in a file marked Warranties, but if you have a lot, consider creating a warranties notebook with pockets for each set of instructions or directions.
- Consider color-coding your files for easy access. For example, you might decide to put all of your household files in red folders.
- Go through your files and clean them out on a regular basis. They will end up too bulky if you never reduce the amount of paper that's in them.

## Tips for Taking Control of Paper

Once you have decided where the paper that invades your life will go, here are some helpful tips that will help you cut down on the amount of paper cluttering your life.

Follow these helpful hints and you are bound to tame the paper tiger at your house!

- Have a master calendar for your family and yourself. I keep a calendar for the family by the telephone and record on it all pertinent events and activities. I also keep a daily planner for myself; in this schedule book I record everything I must do and every place I must go, with condensed lists and notes. In my planner I also have an alphabetized directory of frequently called numbers.
- Discard paper you don't need! Take a look at the paper you save. Message slips? Sweepstakes entries? Junk mail? Coupons? Get rid of any paper that you don't really need. Save the paper you really have to keep and throw out or recycle the rest!
- Handle mail only once. As you open your daily mail, either organize it or discard it. Have a place for each type of paper and immediately put it where it belongs. Here are some examples:

  —*Bills or checks.* Do what needs to be done on them and put them in a specific place to be mailed or taken to the bank.

  —*Invitations.* Write the event on your master calendar, and then put the invitation in a clear plastic envelope in your address drawer to be saved for future reference. If there is a reply card, mail it back immediately.

  —*Junk mail.* Either discard it or put it in the Read Later file.
- Use downtime or spare time to review the Read Later

## GETTING ORGANIZED

file. Take it with you in the car during car pools or to an appointment where you might have to wait.

- Business cards should be placed either in a business card holder or in an electronic address organizer.
- Purchase a Rolodex or an address/telephone organizer and keep it up to date, adding each individual or company you call, fax, or write. File them alphabetically.
- Use a central telephone answering book with carbon copies for office and even at-home use. While this type of book is used mainly in offices and is available at office supply stores, it works beautifully at home, too. Tie a pen on a string to the message book and put it by the telephone that receives the most traffic, and watch how many more messages you will receive. The carbon copy is helpful if you lose the original message after removing it from the book.
- Transfer any telephone number you find yourself calling often from the message book to a master list taped to the back of a cabinet door near the telephone. This saves you time when you are in a hurry and searching for a particular number.
- Create a stationery drawer by your bedside or at your desk. This drawer will be ideal for holding greeting cards, stationery, stamps, and address book.
- Do you save greeting cards, letters, thank-you notes, canceled stamps, invitations? Designate a place for them— for example, a box or a shelf in a cabinet—and put them immediately in that place. I save greeting cards, and each year I go through them and pare them down to the ones that are really close to my heart. I keep them in one

special cabinet and enjoy looking at them throughout the years.

- For important records that must be stored, buy a file box that will be easy to find year after year and create a storage system for the records. Mark the year and what is in the box and put the records in a safe place. Check often to see if you still need them and if they are safe from harm due to the climate.
- Preserve original documents and birth certificates in a metal box or safe. Keep a book that tells you and the family where everything you value is.
- File newspaper clippings or create a scrapbook on a particular topic. Clip the articles and save them weekly in a basket or file, and then choose a time to put them in your scrapbook. Don't let a month go by without tending to this or the articles will pile up.
- Are you a photo fanatic? If you are a photograph hound, then you'll need some help keeping your photographs in order. I found a good album and bought lots of them. Each one is assigned a theme—trips, special events, a specific child—and stored in a closet. I label each album by year and add to them often. For extra photographs, the storage boxes sold at any camera store work best. Also, store special negatives in a fireproof box.
- Consider framing it! I collect picture frames and love framing special articles, photographs, and documents and have decorated our home with many of them. One hall wall and my grandmother's breakfront are filled with framed photographs. When framing photographs, be sure to ask for spacers or use a mat to ensure that the photograph won't stick to the glass.

# GETTING ORGANIZED 41

- Keep a notebook of things to do. Purchase a colorful, easy-to-spot notebook in which to record things you must do, and keep it by your bedside. You can also use self-stick notes for to-do lists, but be sure to refer to them daily and cross off what you have done. If you use a self-stick note, throw it away immediately after doing the activity or deed.
- Consider purchasing a computer. I highly recommend that every home have a personal computer, and I consider mine a vital part of my organizational success. Computers store volumes of information, from important documents to your holiday card address list. They also save you endless time and energy since you can instantly make corrections and avoid having to retype an entire letter or report.
- Create your own cookbook. Some people like to save all their favorite cookbooks and refer to them daily. To save time I have put my favorite recipes in a blank book that was created for making your own cookbook. Some cookbooks even have blank pages at the end of the book so that you can record your own special recipes.
- Keep a magazine basket in your family room or den to hold all of those favorite magazines you haven't read. Once you read a magazine, tear out and file any articles you want to save and pass the publication on to a friend.
- If you plan to save every issue of a particular magazine, purchase an under-the-bed plastic airtight storage box and store them there. Keep them in a dry, cool place.
- Should you get involved in a special project, function,

or fund raiser, buy a notebook just for it, one with pockets designed to hold all necessary information. You'll know where everything is and you'll be better off as time goes by.
- The best way to manage paper is to keep up with it daily and weekly. So make it a mission and get the job done!

# 7

# Special Sections That Need Extra-Special Help!

Many areas of your home and life seem to take on a life of their own when it comes to getting organized. Consider which areas you need the most help with, and then prioritize your approach. Tackle the easiest area first and work your way toward the most difficult.

### Conquer Your Closets

Consider your closets for a moment. Are they attractive? Do they hold everything you need? Or are the clothes crammed together and hard to see? Few closets ever have room left over that is not being used, and in most cases you have to create more space by the process of elimination. So let's get started. Try this exercise: Open your closet door and ask yourself, "Which are my favorite outfits?" Take them out of the closet and decide why you enjoy wearing them. Do you get compliments when you wear them? Do you look terrific in them? Are they comfortable and flattering? Next, look at all the other clothes hanging there that *aren't* your favorites. Why aren't they? Are they outdated? Do they no longer fit you?

Now take everything out of your closet. If you can't bear that thought, then spend a little time at it each day: Try on all your pants one day, all your shirts the next, and so forth. Stick to your mission: Clean out your closet! Keep these rules in mind:

> **Rule 1. If you haven't worn it recently, you must try it on. This doesn't mean holding it up in front of the mirror. You have no idea how it really looks or if it fits at all until you try it on!**

> **Rule 2. If you haven't worn it in one year, consider donating it to a worthwhile cause. If you haven't worn it in two years, definitely donate it to a worthwhile cause!**

### How to Organize Your Closet

There are two possible ways to organize your closet: by clothing article or by color. Both of these approaches work. I like to organize my clothes by color, so I put articles of like color together, while my husband keeps his side of the closet grouped by article of clothing. All his shirts are together, all his pants are together, and so forth. Whichever approach works best for you, go for it!

## Choice 1. Organize your closet by each clothing article.

In this type of organization, all shirts, pants, jackets, blazers, skirts, and shorts are grouped together in your closet. This system makes getting dressed and finding things a breeze. You can also break the clothing areas down by color if you wish, so that like shirt and pant colors are together.

## Choice 2. Organize your closet by color.

In this case, all items of one color are grouped together, so all the pieces of clothing that match are side by side. To further get organized, you can also put like items together, such as all black shirts, pants, skirts, and so on, so that they are next to each other.

### Tips for Conquering Your Clothing Closet

- Choose hangers that match. If every hanger in your closet is different, then all the clothes will hang differently and be harder to organize. Over time, your closet will begin to look like a hodgepodge of hangers. Instead of collecting every variety of hanger imaginable, find inexpensive matching hangers that will function best over time and purchase them in bulk. I use inexpensive white-plastic-coated hangers. Stick to the same style of hanger, and before you know it, you'll have a matching set for every closet.

- Purchase skirt and pants hangers. Also consider buying some space-saving hangers that hold several skirts arranged vertically. Some hangers hold dozens of belts and other hangers are padded for special outfits. Try them—they're terrific!
- Design a master plan for your closet. A closet can be as beautiful as any room in your house! That's right, consider arranging your clothing as thoughtfully as you did your living room. No, you don't have to add wallpaper or artwork, but reorganizing what's in the closet will make you feel really good.
- Organize accessories together. Remember the thematic approach and keep all your belts or ties or handbags together. There are many racks and storage devices that you can install in your closet.
- Organize your best dresses or suits together to facilitate dressing up.
- If possible, get drawers or baskets built into your closet. This might require getting a professional to evaluate your closet space.
- Create a shoe shelf. If room allows, add a shoe rack or shelves built for shoes. Store shoes you don't wear every day in boxes to keep them free of dust. Shoes that you wear every day should be easy to get at.
- Check with your dry cleaner about the best way to clean and store expensive clothing over time. Don't assume anything with clothing you wish to last.
- Short hanging garments can be hung in two space-saving rows. Long hanging garments can be positioned to allow shelf storage above them. Consider all your options and use your space wisely.

## GETTING ORGANIZED

- Check your clothes on a regular basis. If collars are dirty or cuffs are stained, take the items to the cleaners or clean them yourself. The longer you wait to clean most items, the harder they become to clean.
- Last but not least, don't buy something just because it's a bargain. If you don't need it, it's not a good buy. Check your wardrobe every season and update it with basic items only. Give your old suit a face-lift with new accessories. Consider what you really wear most often and then learn from your successes and errors.
- Don't shop until you drop! If your closets are too crowded already, don't go shopping without cleaning out your closet first. Curb your urge to shop by going through your closet for a while. You'll probably discover a few things you haven't even worn!

### Taking Control of Other Household Closets

Many other kinds of closets require attention. Take each closet one at a time, and focus on organizing it. Here are some of the closets that most often need help and some suggestions to start you off.

### Linen Closets
- Sheets are best grouped by size and pattern. Group like sheets and sizes together; for example, all the single sheets should be on one shelf labeled Single Sheets. Keep patterns together so that's it's easy to grab a single top and matching bottom sheet and go.

- Group sheets by the bedrooms they are meant for. If all single flowered sheets or pink sheets belong to one child's room, then group them together. Create a separate stack for each bedroom and you'll save time when making beds.
- Keep towels that are used daily in the linen closet closest to the bathroom they are used in. Consider assigning a single color to each bathroom for easy organization, or buy towels of only one size and color (such as white, which is easiest to match and keep up with over time).
- Check sheets and towels often and retire any linens that are torn or have seen a better day to the laundry room or garage to use for cleanup.

### Toy Closets

- A toy closet should not be a jungle. If your children have too many toys, put some of them away for a while. When you bring the toys back out, they'll be like new again.
- Have a place for everything. Colorful containers make organizing a toy closet easier and are appealing to kids. Stackable bins do a good job holding small objects and blocks, while plastic laundry baskets are great for stuffed animals and dolls.
- Toy closets need extra help on a regular basis. Explain to your children that if they take something out, they must put something back. This helps keep toys from accumulating everywhere.
- Empty the closet out twice a year. Pull everything out

and check it carefully. As painful as it might be to face all of those toys, puzzle pieces, and lost game parts, a thorough cleaning involves checking everything out before it's checked back in.
- Involve the kids. Children of all ages can help clean out the closet and learn the tricks of the trade. Clear containers are perfect for games or puzzles with broken boxes. Grouping like items such as books together helps keep them organized. Children need to be given the responsibility of keeping the toy closet clean. Your guidance will keep them on the right track.
- If the toy closet or toy room continues to be a mess, even after you've tried everything, then make it off-limits for a while.

### Drawers

If your drawers are disorganized, then you need to start from scratch. Take one at a time and don't worry about how many you clean out at first. Cleaning out one drawer might take a great deal of effort, but it's worth the time and energy. Start with the messiest one!

Remove all the contents from a particular drawer. Next, throw out or give away everything in the drawer that you don't need. Have a trash can and a shopping bag by the drawer as you clean it out. Then put back only those things you can use, and be sure to make the drawer really useful. For example, a drawer filled with office materials should be near a desk or a telephone. Think about what needs to be in that drawer, and then plan the contents. Extra supplies should be stored in a separate place, not piled up in the drawer.

## Tips for Getting Your Drawers Organized

- For drawers that hold clothing, group like items together. Have a drawer for socks, lingerie, belts, and so forth.
- Know what's in the drawer. Think about what you need and use most that will be in a particular drawer and then put only those items back in. The drawer should have a specific purpose.
- No junk drawers allowed! If you allow a drawer to be a junk drawer, then that's what's going to end up in it—pure junk. If you have a junk drawer, pull everything out of the drawer and get rid of most of it. If you have five pairs of sunglasses, save only those you really need and wear.
- Place common items that you use regularly in several drawers throughout the house. For example, in a drawer near every telephone put tape, scissors, pens, and a notepad.
- Group like things together in containers, rubber bands, clear plastic bags, or envelopes. Otherwise, they are bound to make a mess.
- When was the last time you cleaned out your drawers? Take a moment and patrol them. Clean them out on a regular basis to avoid a drawer that eventually won't even open! "Clean as you go" should be your motto.
- Purchase drawer organizers to compartmentalize what's

in your drawers. Clear plastic organizers with lined trays are more expensive, but they liven up a drawer and over time will prove well worth the investment. Jewelry drawer organizers have small lined sections to hold each ring or pair of earrings, and the clear, sturdy plastic trays come in a variety of sizes to fit any drawer.

## Cabinets

To maximize the use you get from your cabinets, ask yourself some questions about them. First, what is the function of the cabinet? What will its purpose be over time? What devices are available to increase the space in your cabinet or to make it user friendly? You'll find many options available at stores that carry space-saving devices.

### Tips for Getting Your Cabinets Organized
- Name the cabinet. Define its purpose—for example, a plate cabinet, a pantry, or a household supply cabinet—and stick to that.
- Pull everything out of your cabinet and clean it so that you start with a clean slate.
- Measure your cabinet so that you know your space requirements in case you wish to install additional shelves or gadgets.
- Avoid overloading the cabinet. Are your cabinets fixed permanently to the wall? If you notice any sagging, be

sure to get it checked out. It could mean you've put too much weight in the cabinet.
- Organize the contents of the cabinet by grouping together objects that are alike or related to each other. Don't just pile items in; group them together for easy access according to an organizational plan.
- Make your cabinets visually appealing. The insides of your cabinets should be as attractive as the outsides.

### Extra Storage

Should you run out of closets, cabinets, and drawers and still have lots of things to store, consider alternative spaces that will help you tuck away your belongings in an organized fashion.

### Tips for Successful Storing
- Store objects in sturdy plastic under-the-bed containers, but be sure to know what is in each box and label it. Check the box occasionally to make sure you still feel attached to these items and feel the need to save them.
- Put hooks in walls or use over-the-door hangers for extra hanging space. Over-the-door hangers are especially useful in laundry rooms, by the back door for coats you wear daily, or in clothing closets. There are all kinds of hooks, including decorative racks that hold dozens of baseball caps and odds and ends.
- Don't forget the back of the door. The back of a door

can hold a magazine rack, a laundry bag, or some other storage equipment.
- Utilize empty wall space. Install hanging devices on the walls for a variety of objects, even bicycles and sporting equipment. A grid system works well for many items. Just add hooks and you can hang up almost anything not too big.
- Add shelves of any type, from hanging systems to built-ins. Often extra shelves are all you need. Sometimes shelves are simply too far apart and an extra shelf installed in the middle of the two shelves will give you just the extra storage you require.
- Use colorful hatboxes, baskets, ceramic bowls, or other objects that will add a decorative touch and hold specific items. A bowl in my bathroom holds my makeup, while a large wicker basket in the family room is perfect for all the magazines we like to save. Antique tins and interesting bowls can be used to hold practically anything.
- Buy a plastic bin with multiple small shelves for little things like picture hangers, nails, tacks, needles, and thread. It'll be ideal for holding your odds and ends.
- Now you see it, now you don't! Tables with floor-length tablecloths work beautifully for hiding extra items. Prefabricated wooden tables make excellent end tables or bedside nightstands and are easily dressed up with colorful tablecloths. Hide your extra hatboxes or baskets underneath for an out-of-the-way storage site.

## Family Records, Warranties, and Finances

Keeping your records and finances in order plays a crucial role in getting organized. Know what they all mean, and then know where you put them! Whether you prefer to organize all your records manually or on the computer, always keep an updated backup of your information.

### Create Files on These Categories

Each of these categories should have its own file folder dedicated to it. Each file should be labeled separately—for example, Family Records, Warranties, Finances, etc. We all have our own system for getting this information organized, but be sure to check it yearly. Store the previous year's information in a safe place, and check warranties yearly. Perhaps keep a log that tells you when a warranty is running out.

### Tips for Organizing Your Family Records, Warranties, and Finances

- Alphabetized accordion file folders hold manuals and other items you wish to save. Label the entire folder Warranties for easy organization.
- Have plenty of self-addressed return labels, preprinted envelopes, or an address stamp with your address for making bill paying and all correspondence easier.
- Plan ahead. On your yearly calendar mark specific times to get your finances in order. This works out well when you are preparing to do your taxes; everything is organized ahead of time.
- Create a system for keeping up with everything, from

## GETTING ORGANIZED 55

deposit slips to credit card receipts. Some people like to keep credit card receipts in file folders with the card company's name on it. Deposit slips should be filed for easy access when checking bank statements.

# 8

# The Kitchen

The kitchen is the center of most homes. In our house, the kitchen is the one place we all come together. And so does all of our stuff, from mail to book bags and briefcases. The kitchen is the catchall for our family, as is true for most families. So the kitchen is also one of the best places to get organized.

First and foremost, you must reduce the clutter in the kitchen. Your kitchen should also be organized to simplify tasks done in it. Kitchens need to be clean and lean in order to function well.

So take a deep breath—I mean a really deep breath—and begin with one area at a time. An organized kitchen attracts fewer problems, from dust to pests and unwarranted germs, so make your kitchen a super-organized space. To clean up your kitchen you must first get rid of the things you don't use. To get an organized life you must part with your kitchen clutter, from fancy gadgets to sentimental pot holders.

The one rule I have in my kitchen is to clean up the mess as you make it. I don't wait until I make a huge mess to clean it up. By cleaning as I go, I feel as though I have less to do. Cleaning as I go is now a habit, and it really works. It also allows me to enjoy meals when I know there's not a huge cleanup job waiting for me later.

Here are some tips to help you get your kitchen organized.

### Counters

- Clear off the counters for a clutter-free appearance. This helps your kitchen look its best. It also gives you more room for food preparation, and the work surfaces are easier to keep clean and germ free. Plus, moving and cleaning around objects takes time, so keep the bare minimum on your countertops.
- Keep only what you use daily or often on the counters. Whatever items you use a lot, from the toaster oven to a hot pad, can be left out. Add a decorative touch and they'll be more pleasing. Match a white toaster oven with white counters and choose colorful containers if they need to be left out.
- Get rid of what you don't use. Forget the blender that was a wedding gift. If you haven't used it in years, give it to someone who will enjoy it or save it for a garage sale.
- Choose smaller versions of your electrical kitchen appliances. If you are short on room, check out the smaller-scaled items available, from hand-held mixers to two-cup coffeemakers.
- Decorate with food. Matching clear canisters filled with

colorful pasta and bowls displaying fruit add a wonderful touch to any kitchen and are functional.
- Keep a pad of paper and a pen by the telephone to jot down a note or leave a message for a family member.
- Make sure the area where you do the most food preparation and cooking in your kitchen is clutter-free. These areas need only functional items like a cutting board to be purposeful.

### Refrigerator

- Organize your refrigerator by foods. Keep all the like produce together, breads together, cheeses together, and so forth. This way, if the cheese was eaten up, you'll know by the empty space in your refrigerator.
- Give your refrigerator bins and drawers a specific purpose. Know what goes into each of them, and you'll find it easier to unpack your groceries. Everything you put in your refrigerator should go in a specific spot.
- Clean out your refrigerator before you go grocery shopping and check the expiration dates on food. This way you'll have room for the food you purchase, and you'll also know what you're out of.
- Place the food with the nearest expiration dates up front. Avoid opening two of the same items by using the first one up.
- Keep leftovers in a special place. This way you'll know to keep an eye on them, and if they're not used up, to throw them out.

- Label everything that goes into your freezer and wrap it correctly. Clean out your freezer at least once a month and you will be more likely to use and know what's in it.
- Purchase matching reusable containers that are stackable and fit in your refrigerator. These are great for leftovers, and since they match, you'll have an easier time keeping up with their lids.

### Cabinets

- Arrange each kitchen cabinet with a theme or particular china or glass pattern. Like things should be grouped together and when possible stacked to conserve space.
- Designate a pantry for food and keep it organized. Clean out your pantry so you know what you have, and keep it looking organized. Refer to chapter 4 on space-saving devices and install some extra shelving to hold cans.
- Add shelving to avoid stacking too many cans and objects. Shelving should be spaced to fit what's kept in the cabinet so that you make the best use of space available.
- When organizing your pots and pans cabinet, make sure you have one pot and pan the size of each stovetop element. If you have too many, you'll waste space and never be able to use them all.
- Save room, time, and money by keeping a grocery

list. You'll know what you really need and not shop aimlessly.
- Install adjustable shelves when possible. This will allow your cabinets to suit what's in them.
- Use a lazy Susan for a variety of purposes. Lazy Susans are perfect for spices, cooking needs, and things you use often. Try one out in a cabinet corner or even at the edge of your countertop in case you have shallow cabinets.
- Alphabetize your spices from A to Z. They will be easier to find and this system will save you time.
- If you have young children, install safety locks to keep them from cleaning supplies and other dangerous items.
- To store large trays and platters, install vertical slats or dividers about 4 inches apart. This makes for easy storage and works especially well in a cabinet over your oven.
- Install pull-out shelving wherever you can. This makes for simple storage and easy access. Pull-out shelves are ideal for cookware, pots and pans, and even place mats.
- Tapered glasses that are smaller at the base can be placed in the cabinet with some glasses top up and others top down. More glasses fit in a cabinet this way.
- Use the back of cabinet doors for items such as a paper towel rack, extra shelving, and organizers to maximize space.
- If your kitchen allows, install a work island for extra counter space and added storage.

### Drawers

- Cutlery trays are perfect for storing knives, forks, and spoons. They are even made in a stackable rolling version so that you have two layers, which is perfect for a deeper drawer.

### Dishwasher

- Don't overload your dishwasher. If it's over halfway full, run it and keep up with your dirty dishes. The job will be easier and everything will be cleaner.
- Enlist the family. Everyone can take a turn loading or unloading the dishwasher. Perhaps make it a family rule that dessert comes only after the dishwasher is loaded.
- Create a system to indicate when dishes are clean and when they are dirty. For example, when the dishes are clean, a magnet attached to the door is right side up, and when they are dirty, it's upside down.
- Make it a rule to start the weekend with an empty dishwasher. Dishwashers collect lots of dishes over this two-day, three-night period.

### Other Tips for Organizing Your Kitchen

- If space allows, buy items in bulk.
- Clean as you go. A clean kitchen should stay clean, even if you are making a mess along the way.

# GETTING ORGANIZED

- Install a cordless telephone in the kitchen. You'll be able to cook or clean up and talk at the same time.
- Try to keep small appliances under the counter unless you use them every day. Store them in a nearby cabinet.
- If you don't have sufficient cabinet space, add more cabinets. One extra cabinet can cure a big problem.
- Count the plastic container bottoms and lids you have. Recycle the excess and save only the ones you really need.
- Keep an organized grocery shopping list and stick to it. Plan before you go!

# 9

# Other Areas Around the House

No room escapes the need for being organized. So here are some other areas that need your time and attention.

### The Bathroom

Organizing the bathroom is a cinch. Keep it clean and clutter free and you'll succeed. Stick to the thematic approach when it comes to organizing your drawers, and everything will be at your fingertips. First ask yourself, "What do I use every day?" Have a space and place for those items you use most often, from makeup to your hair dryer to towels and soap.

### Tips to Help You Organize Your Bathroom

- If you prefer that your makeup be left out on the counter, store it in a plastic tray or colorful basket. If you like it in a drawer, organize it so that it's easy to use.
- Designate one cabinet as a medicine cabinet and use a lazy Susan or an organizer to hold the medicine bottles in place. Medicine bottle racks that attach to the inside

of the cabinet door are a great way to save space. If you have young children, be sure to install a childproof cabinet lock.
- Investigate shower shelves and hangers available to hold the soap, shampoo, and odds and ends you need in your shower.
- Keep bathroom cleaning supplies in the bathroom. Make sure they are in a place that's safety locked if you have young children, and keep no supplies in a child's bathroom.
- Keep your toothbrush and toothpaste ready for use in a decorative holder right by the sink.

### The Garage

The garage requires a simple system for getting organized. The one thing most garages have in common is that cars take up most of the space in them. All that's left for storage are walls and corner spaces. With these limitations in mind, you will still find these ideas helpful in getting your garage organized.

### Tips for Organizing Your Garage
- Measure your wall space and install a grid system or some device that holds tools, garden supplies, brooms, and so forth. One system properly installed can last a lifetime!
- Inventory your garage. Know what you own and think about the best way to organize it. If you have many balls and a lot of sporting equipment, then purchase

devices that hold them effectively. Tall wire baskets are great for balls and equipment, while bike racks work beautifully for bicycles.
- Organize your small items—small tools, nails, and odds and ends—in a portable cabinet. Consider purchasing a portable small cabinet that can go anywhere you go! This is an ideal storage system that can move from room to room and is available with rolling casters.
- Install a bulletin board. Your garage can be a space in which to display schedules, children's artwork, and other things you might not have room for in your home. Put one family member in charge of the bulletin board each month to make sure it's updated and neatly organized. Your garage art gallery will brighten a normally dull space.

### The Laundry Room

If you have a laundry room, store in it only those things that help get the cleaning job done. Avoid using laundry-room space as a catchall for everyone's belongings.

### Tips for Getting the Laundry Room Organized
- Install an iron and ironing board holder and use it every time.
- If you have young children, store all cleaning supplies in a childproof cabinet. Designate one cabinet to hold just these supplies.
- Add over-the-door hooks to hold ironed clothing.

- Purchase a laundry rack to hold clothing that you want to air-dry. Fold it up when it's not in use.

## The Basement or Attic

The basement is one of the most disorganized areas in the house. Over half the items we store in the basement are of no value or real use. The climate in most basements and attics often affects the stored items, so check frequently to make sure that what is stored there is unharmed.

### Tips for Getting Your Basement or Attic Organized

- Clean it out once and for all! A basement requires a full cleaning, so start out right and attack it one day at a time.
- Avoid saving boxes unless you really need them. Many basements and attics are filled with empty cardboard boxes. Don't save these boxes, especially the ones from large items such as television sets. If you move, your moving company will wrap large items in moving blankets and strap them in place.
- Time's up! If you are saving records from previous years, don't forget how the years of stored items add up. Decide which records you no longer need and get rid of them.
- Clean up your basement at least once a year. Basements need to be cleaned, vacuumed, and checked for moisture and other problems. Make sure everything you are storing that you care about is safe and sound.

## The Car

Getting organized on the go is very helpful and keeps your car in optimum running condition.

### Tips for Getting Your Car Organized

- First and foremost, do you know where your automobile records are? Make a copy of your insurance card and your car registration for your records and keep the originals in your car. Laminate cards for extra protection.
- If you use your car for business, record the miles in a book. Keep the book and a pencil in your car and be sure to fill it out regularly.
- Follow the instructions in your car owner's manual and have your car inspected as directed. Just because it's running doesn't mean it's perfectly in tune.
- Organize yourself for an emergency. Know what you would do if you had a flat tire or a problem. Consider the options, from a car telephone to jumper cables in your trunk, and be prepared for the what-ifs.
- Keep a tool kit and a first-aid kit in the trunk.
- Keep your car clean with a small battery-operated vacuum on board or a no-eating rule in place.
- Keep a regular maintenance log. Keep up-to-date records of your car's inspections and maintenance visits.
- Make two extra keys. Place one at home in a safe spot and carry the other in your purse or wallet. You'll never regret it if you ever lock your keys in the car. Talk about saving time and money! This really works.
- Keep a trash bag or travel trash can in the car. Don't let

trash pile up. Make it a rule that every time you or anyone in your family gets out of the car, all trash goes with you. The car should not be a dumping ground for everyone's belongings or trash.

- Check out the car organizing devices available, including such great items as change cups, garage door openers, CD or tape holders, trash cans, and over-the-seat organizers.

# 10

# Getting Your Family Organized

Your family will benefit from being organized, and one of the greatest gifts you can give your children besides your unconditional love and time is the gift of organization. The following tips will help your family get organized.

### Focus on Your Family

- Keep a family calendar and have everyone record his or her own important dates.
- Have a family bulletin board to post information.
- Keep a file on each family member.
- Everyone is in charge of his or her own room, bed, drawers, and closets!
- It's everyone's job to help keep your home clean.

### Tips for Helping Your Children Get Organized

- Teach your children how to get organized. Children aren't born with organizational skills, and it takes years of practice and lots of guidance to learn to be organized.

- Make it fun. If kids think getting organized is a bore or a chore, then they're less likely to do it. When planning your child's room, make sure you include organizers for their belongings. Kids need a lot of help getting organized, from pencil holders to drawer dividers to trays for papers and shelves for collectibles. If you dread getting organized they will too, so set a good example.
- Incorporate cleanup games when directing the kids to put away their toys. For example, encourage your kids to be magicians and make the toys "disappear back into the toy closet." Or tell them any toy that's left out will be gobbled up by the toy taker, who keeps toys for twenty-four hours! The toy taker is really a pillowcase with a funny face drawn on it!
- Have a space and a place for everything. Walk through a typical day with your children and involve them in deciding where things will go. Check out their rooms and look for areas that need help, from hooks for jackets and caps to shelves for books and a CD holder for CDs. Remember, there is a way to organize yourself out of every mess.
- Be a clutter buster. Encourage your child to clean out his or her drawers at least once a month. Closets should also be done on a regular basis.
- Hang a shopping bag on the back of the closet door for clothing your children have outgrown and one in the toy closet for toys they no longer want. When it's

## GETTING ORGANIZED 73

full, donate it to a good cause or save it for a garage sale.
- Involve the kids in a garage sale. Refer to chapter 11 on garage sales and let the children play a role. Not only will they see the value of their original purchase reduced, but they'll also see how many things they don't really need and the value of cleaning.
- Involve the kids in keeping their rooms clean. Make this part of being a responsible family member. Everyone is expected to help keep his or her room clean! Praise a clean room and be patient. Organizational skills take time to develop.
- Teach your children how to save time. Doing it correctly the first time saves time, from always putting your shoes in the same place to hanging your clothes in the closet. Help your child understand the importance of putting things away after he or she uses them.
- Praise organization. When your children help or are organized in even the smallest ways, tell them exactly what they did that you appreciate. "Ali, I love the way you organized your notebook and threw the old papers out of your book bag." "Great job! Justin, you made your bed."
- Leave gentle reminders. If there's an ongoing problem and you've discussed it with your child, leave self-stick notes that say, "I'd be all smiles if you clean out your drawer." Make getting organized fun and celebrate small accomplishments.
- Reward small steps towards organization. If your child keeps some part of his room organized or exhibits some organizational skills, reward him or her with a

trip to the store to purchase something for his or her room that will keep things even more organized! You'll be surprised how good you will both feel.

# 11

# Garage Sales

If you really want to get organized, have a garage sale. Consider it as spring cleaning you get paid for! If you've had a garage sale before, then this chapter will help you maximize your earnings. Garage sales take time and effort and requires a lot of energy, but they definitely reinforce your buying less!

### Tips for a Successful Garage Sale

- Plan ahead. A garage sale is more productive if you start early. Hang shopping bags on the back of every door in the house and begin filling them with items that you want to sell. Fill garbage bags with like items—for example, stuffed animals or socks—and store them. Get ready for your sale by checking every drawer, closet, and cabinet. While you might be overly conservative at first, *if you don't use it, choose it* (and sell it)!
- Pick a date for your sale and begin planning. A two-day sale over the weekend works best. Also, have a plan for rain, especially if your sale will be held outdoors.

I prefer a sale held in a garage or enclosed space, but if you don't have such a space, team up with a friend who does.

- Check out your town's laws about such sales. Can you hang signs or is this illegal? Check your insurance and see what liability you have should someone have an accident on your property. Find out what your tax responsibilities are.
- Ask your local newspaper if they have any garage-sale ad specials. Check out the garage-sale listings in the classified ads: which ads would attract you and what about them was appealing?
- Prior to placing your ad, consider what your most attractive items are: silver, antiques, collectibles, small electrical items, garden tools. When placing your ad, be sure to be specific, since your sale is competing with dozens of others. What will make yours more exciting?
- When placing your ad, you can save money by using abbreviations instead of words. Don't be shy with the classified representative. Ask the sales rep for ways to save money on your ad, but be sure to set it apart somehow: use capital letters, spacing, or boldface type for the first few words if you want your ad to stand out from the others. Don't compromise on your ad. It's your best sales tool.
- Be specific about the time of your sale—for example "10:00–4:00 ONLY." Be prepared for early bird shoppers and don't negotiate on your price at the beginning of the sale or everyone there will be bargaining with you.

## GETTING ORGANIZED

- Set up your garage-sale area. Create aisles and set up shopping areas just as you would if you were arranging items in a store. Keep the aisles clear and group things together in an attractive manner.
- You'll make more money at the sale if you display your merchandise in an appealing way. Use tables, hanging racks, and anything that will help your things be easily seen and appreciated. Take your sale seriously.
- Buy sheets of self-stick labels and prepare them beforehand, filling the labels on each sheet with a variety of prices. Then you can move around your sales area pricing items as you come to them, with ready-made labels.
- Put a price on everything, and if you want to sell it, give it a significant reduction from its original price. If you are in doubt, get a second opinion. If you have any antiques, check with an appraiser; you might have something quite valuable.
- Don't reduce items until the last day or few hours of your sale. Tell customers to come back and take their chances. If someone gives you a low offer, take his or her name and telephone number. You'll be glad you did if the object doesn't sell!
- Have one person stay at a check-out table, totally in charge of the money box. Have a lot of change for cash purchases and *never leave the money unattended*. If you don't have extra help, wear a fanny pack.
- Accept cash only. For more expensive items, arrange for a later pickup and request identification. If someone must write a check, get all the relevant information and a local telephone number.

- Use signs to give information that will make the object more desirable. Did someone famous own it? Is it originally from a well-known shop? Is it an antique? If you are offering the item at a huge savings, show the original price. Be a creative merchandiser.
- Make most clothing one price. If everything on the rack is $10.00, your job and the buyer's shopping are much easier. You'll make a little more on one item and less on another, but it simplifies shopping and is a quick way to price things.
- Avoid pricing things under $1.00. Group items that are less together, such as three magazines for $1.00. You can also put them in a plastic bag.
- Involve the kids. They will enjoy being a part of the sale and feel great about the money they earn from their contributions.
- Win some, lose some. Prearrange for a nonprofit organization to pick up whatever you don't sell. Pull the few items you really still love or prefer to save and donate the rest immediately following the sale.

# All's Well That's Organized Well

Now that you have divided and conquered, cleared the clutter and controlled the mess, you probably feel you deserve an award! But take it from me, the rewards will come from organizing yourself, your time, and your space. Once you have gotten a grip on and an understanding of being organized, you'll agree that an ounce of prevention is the key. Now that you're headed down a clutter-free path, you, too, will reap the benefits from a streamlined life and a more organized existence. Life is fuller, richer, and more rewarding when you're organized. Congratulations, you're now on your way!

# Index

Accessories, 46, 47
Appointments:
  scheduling, 2
  writing down, 10
Attics, 68

Basements, 68
Bathrooms:
  organizational themes for, 30
  tips for organizing, 65–66
Bedrooms, organizational themes for, 30
Bill paying, 15
Bins and baskets, 24
Books, 20
Bulletin boards, 67, 71

Cabinets, 5
  kitchen, 60–61
  organizational themes for, 29–31
  space-saving devices for, 25–26
  tips for organizing, 51–52
Calendar, master, 38
Canned goods, 26, 60

Cars, 69–70
Catalog shopping, 12
Children, 71–74
Circular file, 18
Cleanup games, 72
Clear storage containers, 25, 27
Clear-plastic envelopes, 21
Clocks, 9
Closets:
  clothes, 43–47
  hangers, 24, 45–46
  linen, 47–48
  organizational themes for, 29–31
  seasonal cleaning, 21
  toy, 48–49
  uncluttering, 5, 18
Clothes closets, 43–47
Clothing resale stores, 20
Color-coding files, 37
Combining tasks, 13
Computers, 41
Containers, storage, 25–27
Cookbooks, 41
Counters, 21–22, 58–59

Daily planner, 4, 10, 38
Direct Marketing Association, 20–21
Dishwashers, 62
Dividers, drawer, 31
Donations, 18–19, 44, 73
Double hangers, 24
Drawer dividers, 31
Drawers:
 kitchens, 62
 organizational themes for, 6, 29–31
 tips for organizing, 50–51
 uncluttering, 5, 17–18, 49–51
Dry cleaning, 12

Errands, planning, 13
Exercise, 15

File names, 35–36
Filing system, 7, 35–37, 54–55
Food storage, 24
Furniture, functional, 26–27

Garage, 66–67
Garage sales, 73, 75–78
Gift closet, 15–16
Greeting cards, 39–40
Grid system, 25, 53, 66
Grocery shopping, 14

Hangers, 45–46
 double, 24
 over-the-door, 24, 52
Household chores, 11

Important records, filing, 36, 37, 40, 54
In-box, 34
Invitations, 38

Junk mail, 20–21, 38

Kitchens, 57–63
 cabinets, 60–61
 counters, 58–59
 dishwashers, 62
 drawers, 62
 organizational themes for, 29–30
 refrigerators, 59–60

Laundry rooms, 67–68
Lazy Susans, 24, 61, 65
Linen closets, 47–48

Magazine baskets, 21, 41
Mail, 15, 38–39
Meal planning, 13–14
Meal preparation, 14
Medicine cabinets, 65–66
Meetings:
 length of, 12
 writing down, 10
Messages, returning, 11

Organization, (see also Cabinets; Drawers)
 benefits of, 3–7
 clothes closets, 43–47
 linen closets, 47–48
 of paper (see Paper)
 space-saving devices, 5, 23–27

by themes, 6, 29–31
of time, 4–5, 9–16
toy closets, 48–49
uncluttering, 5, 17–22
Out-box, 34
Over-the-door hangers, 24, 52

Paper, 20, 33–42
filing system, 7, 35–37
material and tools for, 34–35
tips for taking control of, 37–42
types of, 33–34
workspace for, 34
Paper towel holders, 24
Paying bills, 15
Photographs, 40
Plastic containers and holders, 25
Plastic-coated shelving, 23–24
Post-it notes, 35
Prioritizing, 11, 14
Procrastination, 11
Professional organizers, 226
Pull-out shelving, 25, 61

Read Later file, 38–39
Recipes, 41
Recycling, 18
Refrigerators, 59–60
Rewards, 13
Rolodex system, 35, 39

Saying no, 14
Schedule book, 4, 10, 38
Scrapbooks, 40
See-through containers, 25, 27
Self-stick notes, 13, 41
Shoe racks, 46
Space-saving devices, 5, 23–27, 60
Stationery drawer, 30, 39
Storage boxes, under-the-bed, 24, 41, 52

Telephone:
answering options, 15
returning messages, 11
shopping by, 12
taking messages, 39
Telephone directory, 10
Themes, organization by, 6, 29–31
Thrift shops, 20
Time, organizing, 4–5, 9–16
Time for self, 14–15
Toy closets, 48–49
Toy storage, 24, 25

Uncluttering, 5, 17–22
Underscheduling, 11
Under-the-bed storage boxes, 24, 41, 52

Warranties, filing, 37, 54

*Divide and conquer your surroundings on your way to a more organized and less chaotic life with . . .*

# KITCHEN 101
## by Robyn Freedman Spizman

Setting up a kitchen can be a daunting job for new home owners and cooking novices. But even so-called veterans can be clueless when it comes to stocking a pantry or determining food freshness. KITCHEN 101 offers quick tips from setup to cleanup, including:

- How to prepare food basics like omelettes, pasta, and baked potatoes
- Which herbs you should always have on your spice shelf
- How to get the most out of your weekly shopping trip
- Ways to get the best use from your microwave or barbecue

Published by Ivy Books.
Available wherever books are sold.